Ladders

SMART ANIMALS

What Are They Thinking?

by Judy Elgin Jensen

The legendary Aesop wrote a fable about a thirsty crow who found a pitcher of water. But the pitcher had a narrow neck and the crow could not fit his head in to drink. What could he do? He picked up small stones and dropped them in the water. As the stones took up space in the pitcher, the water rose higher. Finally, the water rose high enough that the crow could get a drink. The moral of the story? *In a pinch, It helps to use our wits.*

Researchers have found that the intelligence of crows is not a fable! Crows, rooks, and some of their relatives do have "wits" or "smarts." Researchers put a glass of water near some rooks. It contained a worm that was floating too deep in the glass for them to reach. The researchers also supplied some stones. The rooks appeared to analyze the problem before solving it. They studied the container. Then they added several stones without checking to see if they could reach the worm! Once the worm was in reach, they grabbed it and left the testing area. What were the rooks thinking? Dinner!

The Crow and the Pitcher, Rook

SMARTS: Solves problems, uses tools.

New Caledonian Crow

SMARTS: Makes and uses tools to
        find food.

A New Caledonian crow uses a twig to snag a meal.

Have you heard the word "birdbrain" used about someone who has done something not so smart? That person is probably not stupid. Neither are the "birdbrained" New Caledonian crows. The brains of these crows and their relatives are large compared to their overall body size. Humans have this **trait,** or characteristic. So do dolphins and chimpanzees. This trait often means the animal is "smart."

New Caledonian crows seem to be extremely smart, even for crows. These toolmakers make twigs into hooks and tear strips of saw-toothed leaves into spears. With the tools, they snare their favorite foods: grubs and slugs. Often their young are watching.

Unlike most birds, New Caledonian young stay with their parents for two years or more. The family finds food together and family members communicate among themselves. One family's "waak, waak, waak" is often a bit different from the "waak" of another nearby family. The young **inherit** the ability to make tools from their parents but they aren't very good at first. During this time, their parents help them refine their skills. The young start by ripping leaves and fiddling with twigs. At first, the parents dig out a slug or stab an insect for their youngsters to eat. Eventually, the youngsters learn how to make the right tool for the job.

Koko the Gorilla

SMARTS: Uses American Sign Language, makes up new words, paints.

Koko, a lowland gorilla, paints a picture.

Have you made up a name for something when you didn't know the correct word? Koko the gorilla can do that, too. Koko can understand more than 2,000 words (more than most three-year-olds). Even so, she sometimes needs to make up a new word using words she already knows. Shown a mask, she called it an "eye hat." Shown a ring, she said "finger bracelet." Make sense?

Koko, a lowland gorilla, makes a lot of sense. Her vocal cords cannot produce human-like speech, but Koko uses her arms, hands, and fingers to communicate in American Sign Language. Koko can use more than 1,000 signs. She also uses flashcards in conversations.

Dr. Penny Patterson began a four-year study on interspecies communication. It later became her life's work. She teaches Koko and helps interpret the signs Koko has learned and those she has made up. In Koko she has seen both language and emotions. Koko's use of language shows humor, sadness, argument, and moral judgment. Koko paints, and she cries during sad parts of movies. She misses her caregivers when they're gone.

Koko wants to become a mother. The baby would inherit many of its mother's traits, just as all young do. It would have dark fur and small ears. Would Koko teach her baby to sign? Dr. Patterson thinks so. After all, wouldn't you want to be able to "chat" with your offspring?

Alex the Parrot

SMARTS: Counts; knows colors, shapes, and sizes.

Alex, an African Grey parrot, could sort colored blocks.

Alex may have been gray in color but he was certainly bright in smarts! He's so famous for his intelligence that he has a research foundation named after him. Alex died at age 31, which is young for a parrot, but his legacy is lasting.

What did Alex do that was so smart? For one thing, Alex matched more than 100 objects, actions, and colors with their names. For another, he was good at math. Alex could count objects in sets of six. He was working to count sets of seven and eight. He could add sets of objects with a total of six or fewer. He even figured out what "zero" was. Alex could connect a written number, its spoken number, and a set of objects of the same number. He was also learning to read the sounds of letters and beginning to understand how they form words.

How did Alex do it? Through the work and interest of his trainer, Dr. Irene Pepperberg. African Grey parrots have inherited traits that help them imitate many different sounds. These traits include the size of their tongues and a chest structure similar to your **larynx,** or voice box. Wild parrots imitate other species of birds, although researchers do not know how that helps them. In captivity, that can lead to quite a vocabulary!

Elephant

SMARTS: Recognizes self, communicates and
cooperates with other elephants.

An elephant seems to recognize its own reflection. Few animals have that ability.

Like other smart animals, elephants have rather large brains compared to their body size. And they seem to use them! Wild African elephants communicate to keep the herd together. Their low-frequency sound waves can travel a couple of kilometers (more than a mile). They use calls, chemical signals such as odors, and visual cues to tell one another about their environment.

Researchers think elephants in captivity recognize themselves in mirrors. Using a mirror, one touched her trunk to a white X on her cheek but ignored an invisible X marked on the other cheek. Researchers are also learning that elephants are cooperative. A test required that two elephants cooperate to move a slide holding food. One elephant wouldn't start the test if the other elephant could not reach the pull-rope. Elephants have been known to work together to help a fallen elephant get up or to rescue an elephant trapped in the muddy edge of a watering hole.

"Smarts" in animals result from both inherited and learned behaviors. To learn a behavior, animals need to build on inherited behaviors. Living in social groups seems to affect intelligence as well.

It looks like crows heed Aesop and make good use of their wits! But they are not the only ones.

Check In   What connection can be made between brain size and intelligence?

GENRE Science Article

Read to find out about how animals have helped people in some dangerous situations.

DOLPHINS
SAVE SURFER
Page 14

Animals to

by Judy Elgin Jensen

Gorilla Saves Toddler

Sea creatures, African animals, birds of all shapes and sizes, and butterflies abound at Brookfield Zoo near Chicago. In 1996, one three-year-old visitor wanted a closer look at the gorillas. Unobserved, he climbed the railing around the enclosure and fell about 6 meters (about 20 feet) down. He lay still on the concrete floor. What happened next surprised everyone.

A lowland gorilla named Binti Jua, came to the rescue. Bit Binti Jua isn't just any lowland gorilla. She is Koko's niece! Onlookers were sure Binti Jua would maul the boy. Instead she picked him up, cradled him, and carried him over to waiting

Binti Jua holds her daughter Koola. Binti Jua was eight years old when she rescued a boy who had fallen into a zoo exhibit.

paramedics. All the time she carried her own baby on her back. Knowing about Koko, you're probably not surprised. Close relatives can **inherit** similar **traits** that influence behavior.

Zookeepers think two factors contributed to Binti Jua's actions. Raised by humans, she was more

Cell phone cameras did not exist in 1996. A zoo visitor with a video camera recorded the rescue. At the time, Binti Jua became a national hero. Today, videos of the rescue would have gone viral!

"people oriented." Also, the boy was unconscious. If he had been thrashing and crying, he might have seemed like a threat. With prompt medical attention, the boy recovered completely.

Dolphins Deliver!

It was another day at a Monterey, California beach for surfer Todd Endris. He was lying belly-down on his board, waiting for the "right" wave. Then, out of nowhere, came a HUGE shark!

The shark's first attack missed, but the second bite struck Endris's midsection. Teeth on top bit his back, and teeth on the bottom hit the surfboard under his belly. The surfboard kept the sharks teeth from sinking in. The shark slid off, peeling away back skin. In a third strike, the shark's teeth gripped Endris's right leg. Endris kicked the shark's snout with his left leg until it let go.

About 300 teeth in several rows frame a great white shark's mouth.

Dolphins form groups that aid feeding and raising young.

With Endris bleeding badly, the shark was sure to attack again. But a pod of dolphins came to the rescue! They circled Endris until he could steady himself on his surfboard and paddle to where lifeguards waited.

There have been other cases of dolphins protecting humans from sharks. Four lifeguards off New Zealand's shore saw a pod of dolphins barreling toward them. The dolphins bunched the lifeguards together by circling quickly. They were close enough to touch. Then one lifeguard saw the great white shark only 2 meters (about 6 feet) below them. A few years earlier, in the Red Sea, dolphins had also protected humans from sharks by circling them.

Dog Detects Disease

Paul Jackson's blood sugar frequently falls too low. He noticed that sometimes his border collie, Tinker, would bark, lick his face, and cry. Within 30 minutes, Jackson would have a low-blood-sugar attack. Jackson put two and two together. Tinker's behavior was an alert!

Jackson has **diabetes,** a disease in which the body does not break down sugar properly. Some people take a medicine called **insulin** to help keep diabetes under control. But if their blood sugar level plunges too low, they can become confused and lose consciousness. They must smell differently, too. That's how Tinker was able to detect health trouble for his owner.

Many dogs have keen noses. Usually, their sense of smell guides them to food, a favorite toy, or a stray sheep. For a lucky few dog owners, a keen nose is an alert system.

Tinker detected changes resulting from Jackson's particular kind of diabetes. Tinker later became qualified as an alert dog and earned a snappy red jacket.

No human taught Tinker that Jackson's change in smell could be a sign of danger. No human taught the dolphins or Binti Jua to look out for humans. Why would the animals protect humans? Being raised by people may help explain Binti Jua's behavior. It's much harder to figure out the dolphins' actions. They may naturally help protect other dolphins in distress. But it is not clear why dolphins would assist a human in danger.

And Tinker? Well, Tinker is "man's best friend." What would you expect?!

Check In   Describe the unusual behaviors of the gorilla, the dolphins, and the dog. Explain how they assisted each person.

TRAINED TO HELP

by Judy Elgin Jensen

During training, a capuchin monkey is encouraged to use natural behaviors, such as opening a walnut. A walnut is also a tasty treat.

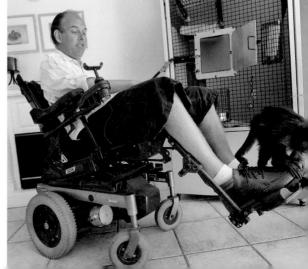

HELPING HANDS
MONKEYS

Capuchin monkeys are native to Central and South America. You might see them scrambling in trees, chattering away, searching for nuts.

But monkeys in the house? Sure, if they are properly trained. **Traits,** such as small size, natural curiosity, and intelligence make them perfect "helping hands" for people who have trouble using their own hands. The monkeys' tiny fingers easily grasp small objects. The monkeys can be trained to turn on light switches, pick up dropped phones, load a DVD, or fetch a jar of peanut butter.

Training begins with just a few toys. Trainers shine a laser light on an object to focus the monkey's attention on it. When the monkey responds, trainers reward it with praise and food. The monkey knows it did the right thing. Simple commands help guide the monkey, too. Gradually, more and more items are added to the monkey's environment. Eventually it looks like a small apartment.

The trained capuchin monkeys get along well with people. After a while, the monkeys can even predict what their human companions need next! Capuchins live for 30–35 years, so they can help owners for a long time. But monkeys aren't the only smart animals people train. Let's find out about some others.

Helping hands monkeys can use a cloth to help scratch an itch. They can also move a foot rest, flip a switch, or turn a page for their human companions.

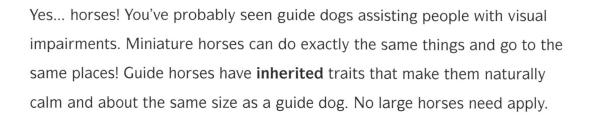

GUIDE HORSES

Yes... horses! You've probably seen guide dogs assisting people with visual impairments. Miniature horses can do exactly the same things and go to the same places! Guide horses have **inherited** traits that make them naturally calm and about the same size as a guide dog. No large horses need apply.

Why would someone choose a guide horse? One big reason is life span. Horses live as long as 40 years. If you got a guide horse at age 16, you could be over 50 before it died. In that time you might need three guide dogs. Horses can start guide training as young as 6 months. They have hundreds of training hours before they are ready.

Miniature horses can be trained to stay quiet in noisy places. With eyes on either side of their head, horses can see almost all around in a full circle. One eye can look one way while the other can see danger in a different direction.

Guide horses offer another option to people who need help because of vision problems.

Horses also seem to have good memories. They can travel great distances and don't get excited when petted.

Guide horses can live inside, but prefer to live outdoors. They don't mind the cold and they do well inside small barns. A fenced, grassy area is a good environment. People who know their own homes very well but need help once outside might find a guide horse the perfect companion!

A guide horse might help with everyday tasks such as retrieving keys.

When off duty, a guide horse exercises outdoors.

A trained guide horse is not distracted in public places.

A guide horse locates the exit from a school building.

RESCUE DOGS

In 2010, a devastating earthquake struck Haiti. Within hours, a border collie named Hunter and his handler reached the site. They joined dog-human teams from around the world. Hunter crisscrossed the rubble, sniffing for survivors. "Here!" he barked. Three girls were under the broken concrete. Without Hunter's highly-trained nose, they would have died.

Disaster search teams like Hunter and his handler seek survivors in storms, mudslides, explosions, and wrecks. Search dogs easily move on unstable surfaces and crawl through tiny spaces. They respond to spoken commands and hand signals. The work requires more than a keen nose. These dogs need strength, speed, and high energy.

An earthquake victim might survive a few days, giving teams time to search. A skier buried in an **avalanche** needs help within minutes. Avalanche search

Good training and super swimming abilities are needed for a successful water rescue.

dogs move quickly. They can search an area the size of a football field and find a person trapped under 3 meters (about 10 feet) of snow within 30 minutes.

Jumping from a boat can be a water rescue dog's idea of fun! A dog's natural love of water helps in this work. Newfoundland dogs make good water rescue dogs. Webbed feet and strong muscles help them swim. Thick fur keeps them warm in cold waters. They can tug a person to shore, tow a small boat, or keep a victim afloat while a human revives the victim.

A German shepherd works quickly. There is no time to spare when searching for avalanche survivors.

A rescue dog searches for people trapped in rubble.

A fire service dog and handler practice rescue techniques.

Dogs that assist police must learn to follow instructions reliably.

BEAGLE BRIGADE

You've just flown back home from another country. You wait for luggage and see a little dog running around the bags. Suddenly it stops and sits quietly by one. A uniformed agent comes over and searches the bag. What's the problem?

Many people accidentally bring plant and animal materials into the country. The materials might harbor seeds, diseases, or pests that can cause problems. Sometimes people try to sneak in these materials!

Beagles are naturally good at sniffing and tracking prey. During two years of training, they learn to distinguish odors of meats, fruits,

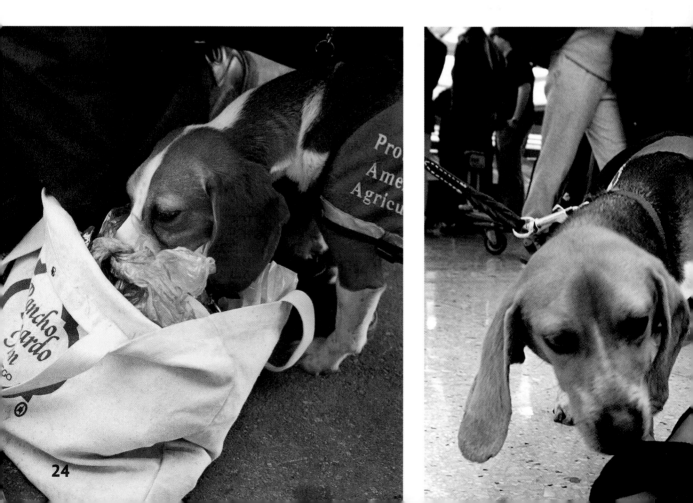

and other materials. Experienced dogs can sniff out illegal materials 90 percent of the time. Their sniffing keeps 75,000 illegal items out of the country every year!

Certain traits help animals succeed in their jobs. Training builds on inherited behaviors and traits to develop the right skills for a job. For some, such as the beagles, work seems like a fun game to get treats. Others, such as rescue dogs, work for the praise of their human partners.

More than 220 million scent receptors line a beagle's nasal passages. A human has a measly 5 million receptors.

Check In How do inherited traits help determine the work for which an animal can be trained?

TREATING ANIMALS RESPONSIBLY

by Joe Baron

Some animals do amazing things, such as a gorilla that uses American Sign Language to express its emotions. To people who study, train, or enjoy being with animals, it is important to treat them ethically, or with great care. Ethics are personal ideas of right and wrong that guide how we treat others. But everyone, not just animal lovers, should treat animals well. Read on to see reasons for people to treat animals responsibly.

Zoos

Treating animals responsibly helps keep them healthy. Exhibits at the Taronga Zoo in Sydney, Australia, are designed for the well-being of animals. At the zoo, a Kodiak bear digs into a piñata filled with its favorite foods. A western lowland gorilla forages and finds a container of popcorn. Elephants wallow in mud, just as in the wild. Mud cools them and protects their skin from sun and insects.

Many years ago, most zoos looked very different than they do today. Animals were in cages. They were given food, water, and little else. Today, many zoos provide interesting and natural habitats for animals. They allow animals to experience natural behaviors. The animals dig in soil, forage for food, sniff scented plants, climb, play-hunt, problem-solve, and socialize.

Places like the Taronga Zoo aren't just good for the animals. They're also good places for people to observe and learn about animals.

At the Taronga Zoo, a male Asian elephant plays with a bungee ball while a female elephant steps into a dirt bath.

Wildlife Refuges

Treating animals responsibly helps preserve ecosystems. Governments and private groups around the world set aside land and water for wild animals. The word **refuge** means "to be sheltered from danger." Wildlife refuges provide space for animals to live without people hunting them.

The National Elk Refuge in Wyoming was one of the first big refuges in the United States. In the early 1900s, farmers started living on the same land the elk used in winter. With less space in hard winters, thousands of elk starved. So people worked with the government to set aside about 700 hectares (1,760 acres). Today the National Elk Refuge is about 9,700 hectares (about 24,700 acres) and supports 5,000–8,000 elk in the winter. Bison, wolves, bighorn sheep, and migratory birds also use the refuge. And all this sits right beside a city! In fact, the refuge is good for the city because it attracts visitors. It also provides natural beauty that the community values.

The National Elk Refuge was set aside near Jackson Hole, Wyoming in 1912.

The Ngorongoro Conservation Area in the United Republic of Tanzania was set aside in 1959.

The Ngorongoro Conservation Area is in central Africa. It spans vast plains, savannas, and forests and protects many kinds of animals. It also allows a local people, the Maasai, to raise their grass-eating livestock. More than one million wildebeest migrate through the area in search of food and water. So do zebra and gazelles, and their predators—lions and hyenas. People come from around the world to see the wildlife. They spend money that helps the local economy.

Saving the Rhinos

Treating animals responsibly helps prevent them from dying out. Cutting off a rhino's horn might kill it or save its life. It depends on who's doing the cutting. **Poachers,** or illegal hunters, kill rhinos for their horns. They don't care if the rhino lives or dies. People have used the horns to carve cups, buttons, and other objects. Some people believe the horns make strong medicine, but scientists have not proved it. Many people will pay a LOT of money for a horn that weighs about 3.5 kilograms (8 pounds). South African law allows hunters to take the horns out of the country legally. But the horn must be a "trophy," which means that the animal must be dead. Many horns are taken out illegally, too.

It's a different story if an ethical person cuts off the horn without harming the rhino before a poacher can find the rhino. A shot knocks out the rhino instead of killing it. A power saw is used

to cut off the horn a little above its base. Rhinos use their horns mainly to frighten or impress other rhinos. So is a hornless rhino at risk? Most people don't think so. They say the rhino's size, strength, and speed will protect it without the horn.

One rhino "farmer" says cutting off a rhino's horn is just like shearing sheep for wool. The rhino horn will grow back in about two years. He thinks it's a good thing to do because it may keep poachers from killing all the rhinos.

There's one more reason to treat animals responsibly. It is simple, but profound. People should treat animals well because many animals are thinking, feeling creatures. So think about it. How can you make sure animals are treated well?

A rhino might take 20-30 minutes to wake up after its horns are cut off. The procedure doesn't cause any pain.

Check In Compare and contrast the ways the different groups are treating animals responsibly.

Discuss

1. What do you think connects the four pieces in the book? What makes you think that?

2. Think about and describe three ways that animals show that they are "smart."

3. Compare "Animals to the Rescue" and "Trained to Help." How are the actions of the animals in these two pieces alike and different?

4. What are some inherited traits that make miniature horses suited to be trained as guide horses?

5. In "Treating Animals Responsibly," what are some reasons that people should care for the well-being of animals?

6. What do you still wonder about intelligent animals and treating them responsibly? How can you find out more?